On Tour with Renzo Piano

Gift of John Bowyer

Contents

Introduction

Renzo Piano's contribution to architecture is recognized internationally just as his achievements are on a global scale. Indeed, he has often cited the very concept of travel as the inspiration as well as the means of his work.

Since he graduated in 1964, his career has taken him to all corners of the globe, on projects and worksites that have included museums, factories and urban renewal. This focus was established from his early key commission for the Centre Georges Pompidou in 1971, working in partnership with Richard Rogers, when he discovered Paris. Since then, he has retained an office there, in addition to Punta Nave, Italy. These are the two centres of his world, from where he travels to places as far as New Caledonia in between.

A spirit of adventure pervades each project by the Renzo Piano Building Workshop, wherever it may be, whether small or large in scale. It is this spirit, found in each preliminary sketch and followed through to each realization, that finds its expression through constant exploration, as each project pushes boundaries, explores new technologies and takes on new challenges. Such are the characteristics for which Renzo Piano is particularly recognized. It is in celebration of this spirit of architecture that Piano repeatedly embarks on a new journey, and which is expressed in his work from early sketch to masterplan, from the design of each structure to each tiny detail.

The experimentation for which Piano is recognized is also an expression of more personal beliefs and experiences. From his father, a building contractor, he observed the builder's responsibility to give special attention to every detail and as a result that architects could be concerned with more than aesthetics. This in turn established a desire for collaboration and for an interdisciplinary approach to architecture. Each project brings together a group of professionals from various fields: engineers and technical specialists, landscape designers and anthropologists, or even musicians and art specialists. Through travel he meets the widest range of people, rooted in different cultures, customs and places.

This book is a tour: it allows the reader to travel together with Renzo Piano around twenty-two of his realized projects. It offers the rare privilege of a guide through the eyes of the architect, focusing not only on what are the key elements of each building, but also on how each is perceived by its originator. Presented though introductory text, a concept sketch and a sequence of photographs that take the reader from the outside to the inside, from overview to detail, the diversity and original accomplishment of each built project is revealed.

If there are recurring themes, these find expression perhaps in a predominance for projects with cultural significance. A passionate lover of music, especially contemporary music, Piano has designed spaces where music is the main protagonist, making concerts and performances a unique experience for the audience, such as in the 'Parco della Musica' Auditorium in Rome or the Niccolò Paganini Auditorium in Parma, Italy.

Piano has also carried out extensive work on the natural illumination of exhibition spaces, such as the Menil Collection, the Cy Twombly Pavilion, and the Nasher Sculpture Center, all in Texas, USA; the Beyeler Foundation in Basel, Switzerland; and the Giovanni and Marella Agnelli Art Gallery at Lingotto, in Turin, Italy. Each project provides a solution in the form of a new, unique roof structure which was elaborated, carefully and slowly, with the help of museum experts and light engineers.

Other projects with a cultural bias include the Jean-Marie Tjibaou Cultural Center, in Nouméa, New Caledonia, where the natural world is used to express the poetry of the Kanak customs and to provide its context.

Scale is another fascinating feature of Piano's work. If some projects are so small that they are designed for quick dismantling and resurrection on a regular basis, such as the IBM Travelling Pavilion, others are so large in scale that they are almost impossible to grasp, such as Kansai International Airport Terminal, Japan, or Potsdamer Platz Reconstruction in Berlin, Germany. While projects can vary so much in their concept and scope, what binds them together is their attention to detail. For this is the lasting impression of each project, and it has come to be the approach of the Renzo Piano Building Workshop.

Although it spans more than three decades of his career and is organized chronologically, *On Tour with Renzo Piano* does not offer the experience of travelling in time. And although the reader will visit many countries, it is not a world tour. This book is rather a series of mini-tours of various projects. The aim is not to work out a global philosophy or a systematic rule for his approach to architecture or aesthetics, but to allow certain aspects of Piano's body of work to find a natural expression in such a personal publication. This book, in short, is a trip into the world of architecture, the passion of a man and the life of one of the major architects of our times.

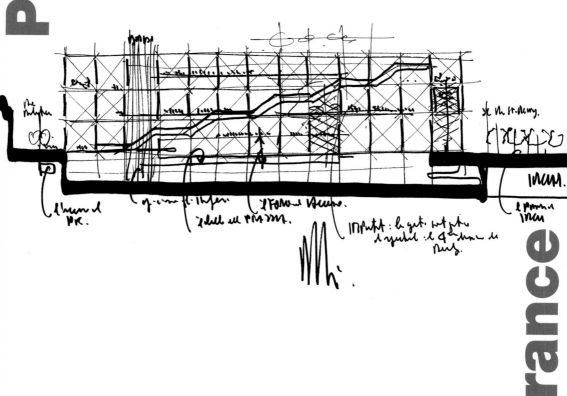

Centre Georges Pompidou

The Centre Georges Pompidou gave my life and career a decisive turn. Both for my friend and then partner Richard Rogers and for me it was a challenging, fascinating architectural and human adventure. We were both young, quite idealistic and certainly provocative architects, who entered a public competition to design a cultural centre right in the middle of Le Marais, the most ancient part of Paris, just a short distance from Notre-Dame Cathedral. Paris has been my second home town ever since: I kept the office we set up for the site, and I now commute between there and my Genoa studio.

The building we had in mind was non-traditional in appearance and concept. We wanted all the space inside to be dedicated to arts, literature and culture, and so we collected all the building's services outside. Since we had to show these functions, we decided to do it in a colourful way: red representing vertical means of transport, yellow for electrical cabling, green for fluids, blue for air ducts and air-conditioning, and white for the structure.

We liked to refer to it as a vertical village, a place where tourists, students, passers-by and Parisians could mingle, come to enjoy the view over the city, visit exhibitions, read or linger. When going towards the top of the Centre on the external escalator, the view extends from the piazza to the Marais area, gradually embracing all of Paris. This is an extraordinary experience, and in more than thirty years I have never grown tired of it. One of the main parts of the project was the gently sloping piazza, a popular meeting place where people gather along with the Centre's visitors, making a perfect audience for the many buskers and actors performing there.

The project caused a huge intellectual controversy at the time, but it was significant that Parisians soon started calling it simply 'Beaubourg', after the area within Le Marais. This was the first 'piece of city' I had helped to create, and it was certainly a great incentive to carry on.

9

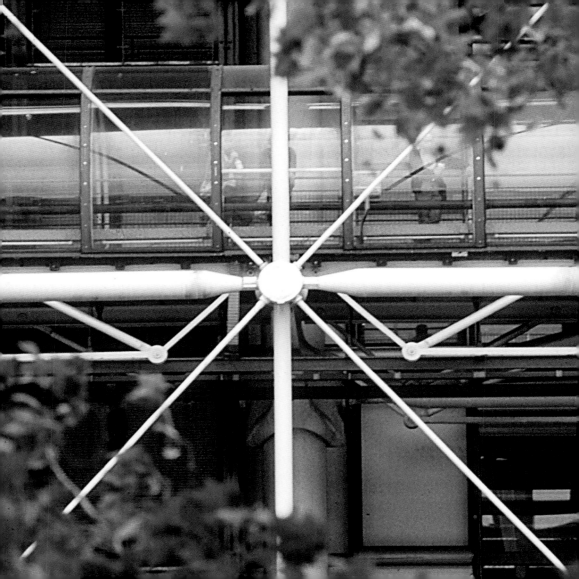

Paris

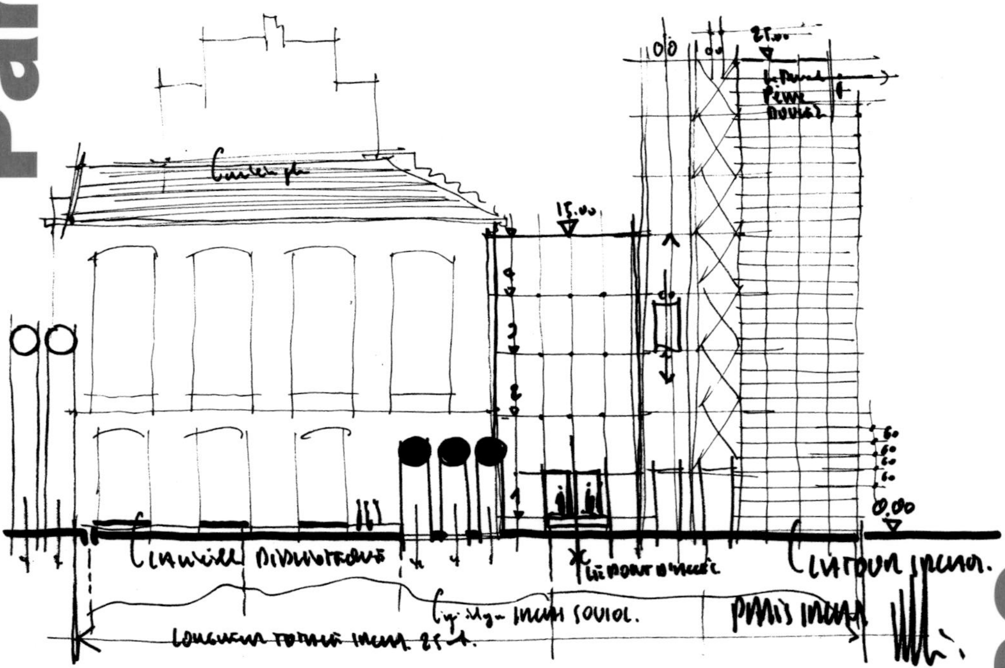

France

IRCAM

IRCAM (the Institute for Research and Coordination of Acoustics and Music) is part of the Centre Pompidou. Although its first phase was conceived and built at almost the same time, IRCAM constituted an adventure on its own, and a first contact with the architecture of music.

Standing on a corner of the Beaubourg piazza, and mostly underground, IRCAM has a narrow flagship office building, with a glass- and terracotta-panel facade. It overlooks the Place Stravinsky and a joyful, colourful fountain with sculptures by Nikki de Saint-Phalle and Jean Tinguely. The visible tip of the iceberg, the above-ground high-rise is a recent addition to the site, completed in the late 1980s. Terracotta has a simple, stylish texture, adding to the chromatic and architectural variety of the area.

IRCAM exists in the realm of contemporary music, a fascinating discipline at the crossroads of music, architecture, mathematics and acoustics. Its first director, Pierre Boulez, made me discover and love an art and a world I had hardly suspected before. He turned out to be an invaluable guide to the strict requirements of acoustics.

We enter IRCAM from the Place Stravinsky, across a tiny bridge over glazed light-wells illuminating parts of the underground structure. A simple issue of space meant that IRCAM's music spaces had to be built below ground. Their location also helps to reduce as much as possible noise and vibration intruding from outside. As in many of our 'musical projects', the space adapts to the music, rather than the other way round.

A great deal of acoustic research is done at IRCAM, where researchers, musicians and engineers work together. Modular ceilings and walls are covered with prismatic forms in relief, which, according to their position, change reverberation characteristics. Eight special music rooms include one large recording and public hall and three teaching and research halls. There is also a state-of-the-art recording studio. IRCAM's futuristic appearance expresses the avant-garde nature of its purpose.

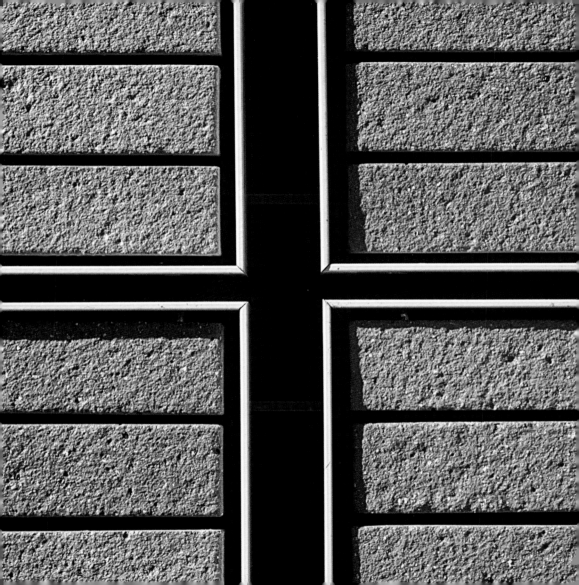

Paris

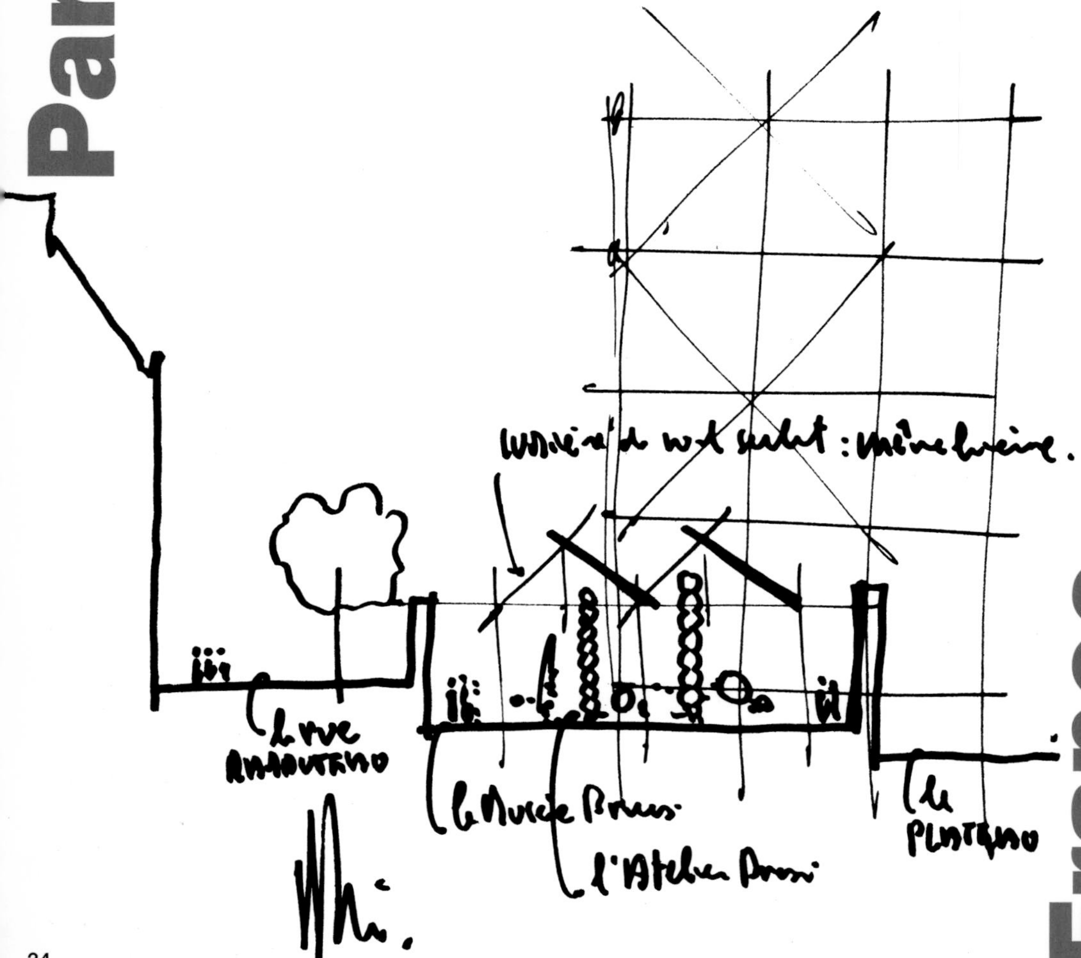

France

Atelier Brancusi Reconstruction

When the Centre Georges Pompidou opened its doors in 1977, I did not think it would affect my life so much. I thought I would return to the area as a visitor. It turned out that I often came back for professional reasons.

IRCAM, the first satellite project on the piazza, was conceived almost at the same time as the Centre itself, but the second, the reconstruction of Romanian artist Constantin Brancusi's studio, started years later. Building such a small project in the shadow of a very big one does not necessarily mean it is simpler. Reconstructing the studio was not easy as it required complete faithfulness to the legacy of the artist. Brancusi (1876–1957) bequeathed all his work to the French State at his death, on condition that it remained in the place in which he created it. The insalubrious area in which it was located, outside the centre of Paris in the 15th arrondissement, had to be demolished, but the State kept its promise: Brancusi's work was to be displayed in a museum especially built for it, resembling the original space as much as possible.

If its location is different, the reconstruction remains faithful to the size, space and general arrangement of the original workshop. Though small, Brancusi's studio is intended to be luminous: the museum is open on two sides thanks to large bays and glass entrance doors. These openings, contrasting with the thick, light-coloured stone walls, help to make the tiny space light and cosy rather than cramped. The partly glazed roof structure recalls the shape of typical Parisian workshops.

Inside, in the middle of two large rooms, works of art (mostly large wood or stone sculptures), tools, various creations and possessions of Brancusi are set out as they were in their first home. Respecting the disorder favoured by the artist has recreated the genius loci, the spirit of the place.

Locating Brancusi's studio in the centre of Paris gives this prolific artist the audience he deserves. The intimate atmosphere of the place is closer to that of the home of a creative genius than to a traditional museum. 35

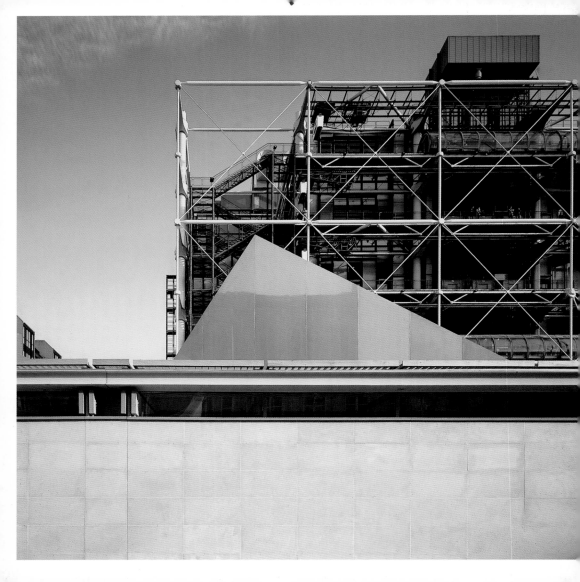

46

The Menil Collection

Art collector Dominique de Menil counts among the most important people I have met in my life. A soft-spoken, discreet, yet passionate woman, she was also extremely determined in her idea of having an experimental museum built to house her primitive- and contemporary-art collection. This was our first major project in America, and a valuable introduction to the use of natural light in artistic contexts.

The Menil Collection lies in a luxuriant park in central Houston. A simple single-floor structure, it borrows the 'balloon-frame' principle and wooden facade of traditional American clapboard housing, and of the museum's immediate neighbourhood. On top of this single floor, we created the 'treasure house', a storage area, narrower than the museum but equally long, which seems to be simply laid on a small section of the roof. In this climate-controlled section of the building, parts of the rotating collection are stored while waiting to be displayed. Natural light as the main source of illumination inside the galleries was one of Madame de Menil's major demands. After much studying with a team of engineers, we came up with the design of a special roof structure, made up of a series of parallel ferro-cement 'leaves'. These let the light pour in while controlling damaging sun rays.

Ground-floor spaces are dedicated to housing the exhibition, and also to a restoration workshop that has a major role in the museum's function too. When we enter the museum, we are touched by the simplicity. Internal garden and glass panels create multiple visual layers inside the galleries. White walls, dark wooden floors and the beautiful light all contribute to make this a contemplative space, where works of art are the centre of attention. These features, together with the use and repetition of multiple plans, add to the feeling of space and luminosity in the gallery. This was what both Madame de Menil and ourselves strived to achieve: the space adapts itself to its artistic content and not the other way round. Success in meeting that challenge owes a lot to her, and what we experienced and learnt here has had a large impact on subsequent projects.

47

Houston Texas

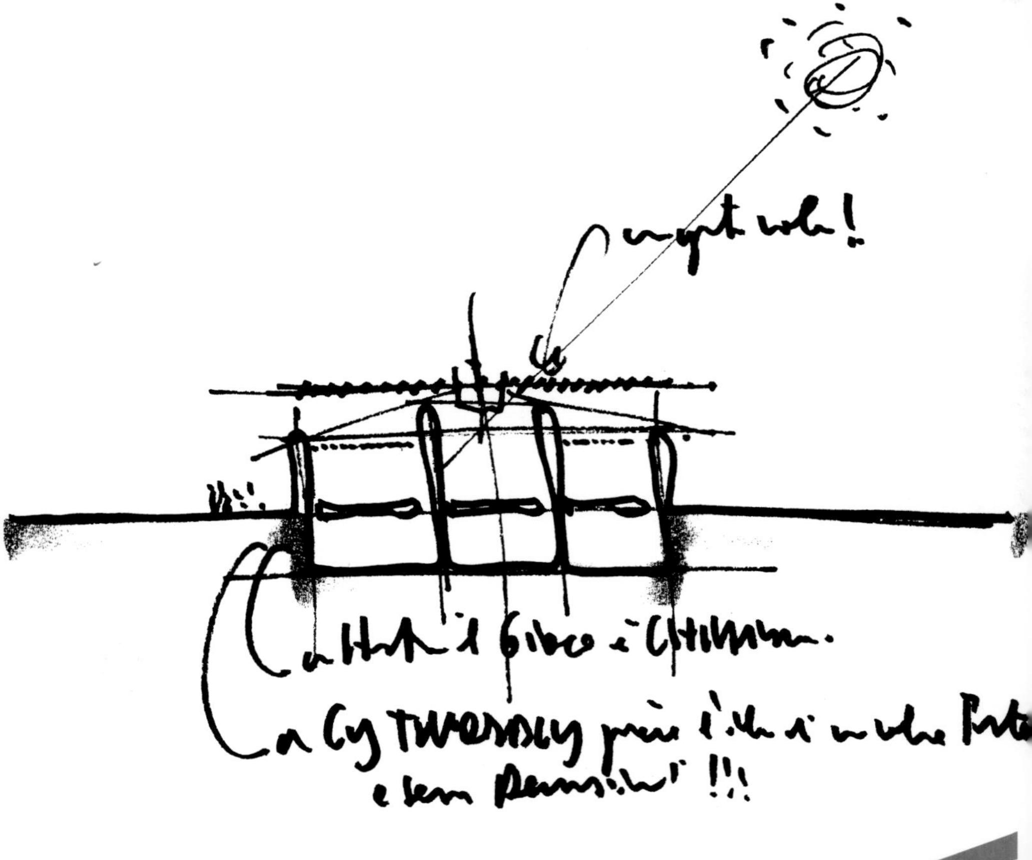

USA

Cy Twombly Pavilion

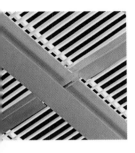

A few years after completion of the Menil Collection, Madame de Menil expressed the wish to have another structure built. Its purpose was to exhibit permanently the work of American painter Cy Twombly (b.1928). The pavilion was to be located in the precincts of the Menil Collection, the gallery she first commissioned, located in a park in downtown Houston. Both projects, however, were to be structurally and architecturally independent. Working again with Madame de Menil was a thrilling prospect and pleasure, and an opportunity we were quick to accept.

Naturally, Cy Twombly was involved in the creative process, and he expressed only one condition: the structure had to be kept as simple as possible, in its shape, appearance and materials.

From the outside, the pavilion is a simple single-floor structure. Its external walls are covered in large cream-coloured precast-concrete blocks. A major characteristic of the project is the roof, a flying-carpet structure, seemingly levitating over the pavilion itself. However, its function differs from the roof we conceived a few years before for the Menil Collection: it filters out more sunlight.

The natural light inside the pavilion is complemented by more constant artificial lighting. It pours into the square-shaped museum, itself divided into nine smaller squares of equal size, each acting as a gallery. This was another requirement of the artist himself, stressing the scope of Twombly's paintings. Features such as white walls, light wooden floors and side openings reinforce the essential feeling of overall simplicity.

This project, although carried out in close collaboration with Madame de Menil, was designed for the work of one living artist, which is rare. The building is made-to-measure, and therefore mirrors not only his personality, but also that of his creations. This is why the Cy Twombly Pavilion is autonomous to the Menil Collection.

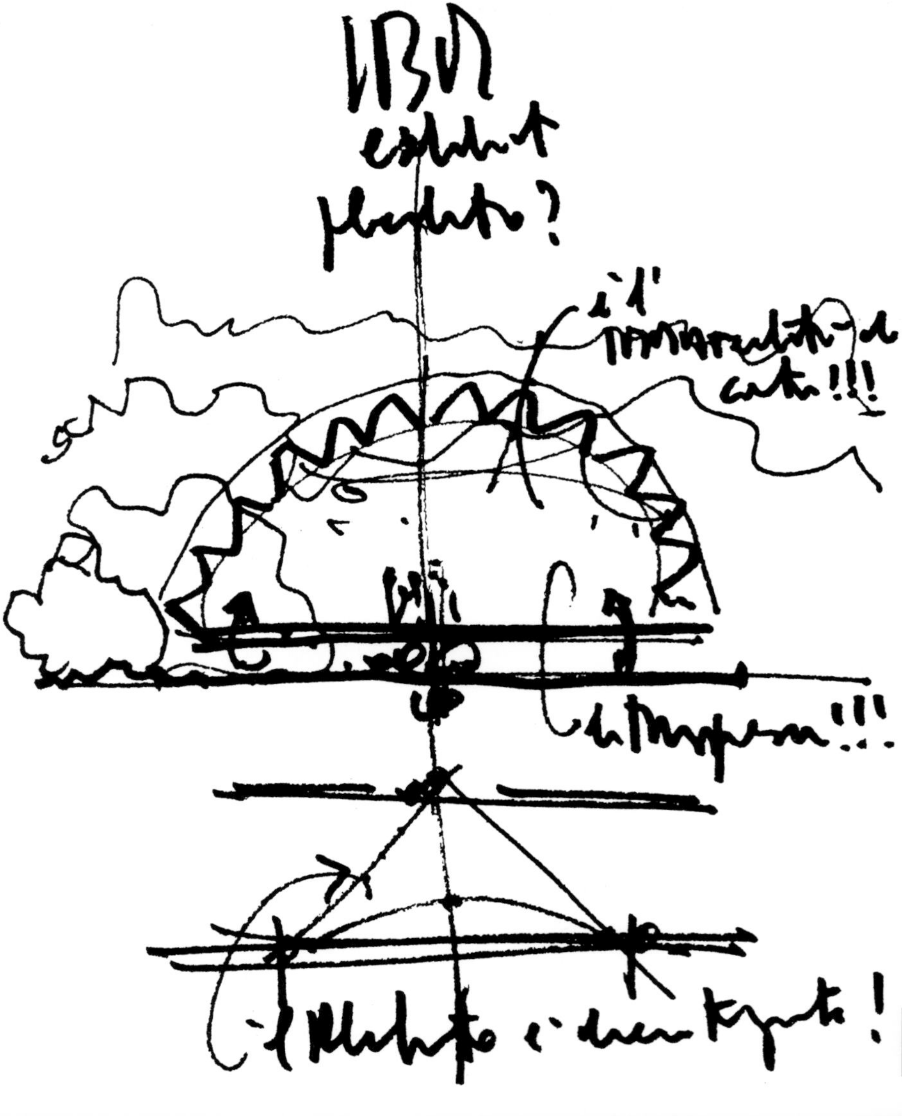

IBM Travelling Pavilion

In the early 1980s, computers were available to a limited number of people – mainly because of the complicated technology of the software at the time. IBM decided to organize an exhibition travelling across Europe, trying to explain the future of telecommunication and computing technologies, and how everybody's lives could benefit from them. In keeping with this spirit of discovery and progress, IBM asked us to design a special pavilion that could face successive assembly and disassembly. The result was the equivalent of a technological circus tent.

The pavilion toured many of Europe's principal cities, north to south, east to west, for three years: inhabitants of major cities – among them London, Rome, Paris and Copenhagen – had a chance to discover the exhibition and its mobile home. It was installed in various locations, such as parks, squares and even once on a crate floating on a river: whatever its temporary environment, the IBM Pavilion seemed to integrate perfectly with its surroundings, either architectural or natural.

Because the structure was a temporary one, it offered lots of space for experimentation, especially as far as the general shape was concerned, and new materials (such as ultra-strong adhesive) were used, which are fine for such a shortlived building. This half-cylindrical structure (48 x 12 x 6 metres/157 x 40 x 20 feet) was constructed of forty geometrically uniform arches made of laminated wood with cast-aluminium joints and a series of identical polycarbonate prisms that acted both as the overall covering of the structure and as windows. They gave the whole pavilion not only a very light and luminous look but also a futuristic appearance that was in keeping with the philosophy of the IBM exhibition.

The pavilion was a clamorous success at the time but it was decided from the start that it would be destroyed at the end of the exhibition. Photographs and drawings are therefore the only tangible souvenirs of this exciting adventure.

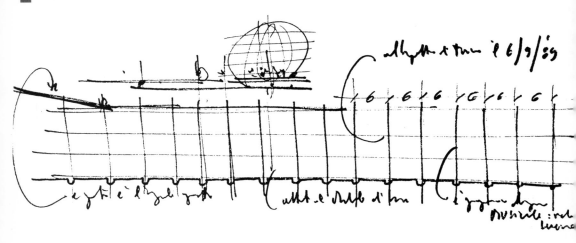

Lingotto Factory Conversion

Lingotto, the historic Fiat factory, represents one of the early 20th century's finest examples of industrial architecture. It is also highly symbolic of the city of Turin and of Italian industry. We faced a new challenge, almost as huge as the Lingotto itself: giving a second life to a 500 metre (1,640 foot) long, five-floor reinforced-concrete structure, enclosing more than a million cubic metres. The intention was noble, and Fiat's then President, Giovanni Agnelli, turned out to be the perfect client. A fascinating personality, dedicated and trusting, he had many ideas for his beloved Lingotto. He followed every stage of the renovation closely, from the launch of the project in 1983 until his death in 2003.

The new Lingotto constituted a gift from Agnelli to his home town. His goal was to turn it into a new piece of Turin, using all the available space for activities lacking in local life. Its function was more than simply filling an empty space. A multi-purpose cultural and leisure area, a shopping centre, a conference hall and auditorium found a place in the renovated complex, as well as a hotel, various offices and a section of the university. We overcame the original difficulty set by its monumental nature; new functions were found and people eagerly adopted them (including the signature roof-track, now a popular promenade).

Overlooking the complex, a bubble-shaped meeting-room for Fiat's board of trustees stands on top of the South Tower, one of the transverse buildings of the complex. A light glass structure, apparently floating over the Lingotto, it offers people inside a wonderful view over the building, the area, and over Turin and the neighbouring Alps. The bubble and its counterbalancing heliport can be seen as symbols of the Lingotto's new look and life.

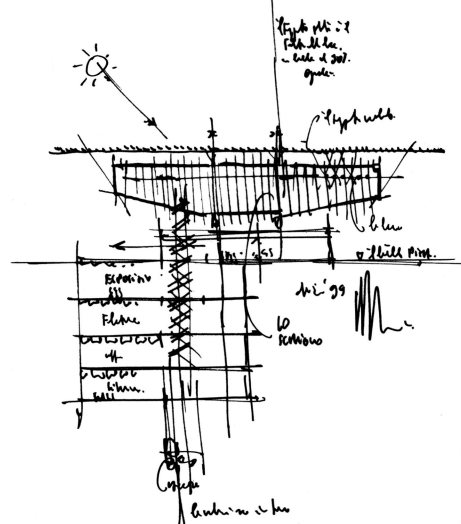

The Giovanni and Marella Agnelli Art Gallery at Lingotto

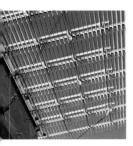

Fiat's former President, Giovanni Agnelli, who commissioned the Lingotto renovation, and his wife Marella were fervent art collectors. Wishing to make public a part of their collection, they asked us to design a small museum within the Lingotto. This gallery would add to the overall conversion, as well as to its multi-disciplinary purpose.

Located on top of the South Tower, the Giovanni and Marella Agnelli Art Gallery, a 2,800 sq. metre (30,128 sq. foot) 'project within the project', has a dual structure. The first is what Agnelli liked to refer as the Scrigno, the 'Treasure Box', a sanctuary where the permanent exhibition is displayed. Entirely made of steel, almost without side-openings, the foundry-shaped gallery stands on four spider-like feet, seeming to float above the Lingotto, thanks also to its 'flying-carpet' roof structure. Below the gallery, and linked by suspended staircases and a panoramic lift, three floors of the South Tower have been turned into temporary exhibition spaces.

The Scrigno can be entered either from the Lingotto's bottom floor or from the roof-track. Inside, the experience is almost religious. The space, deliberately kept small (just 450 sq. metres/4,842 sq. feet), has thoroughly simple, pure settings: white walls, a wooden floor, and the natural light pouring from the roof (which can be regulated by a system of shutters). Admiring the collection of work by Pierre-Auguste Renoir, Pablo Picasso, Antonio Canaletto, Amedeo Modigliani and others in such conditions adds to the general experience of beauty.

The 'Treasure Box' is counterbalanced by the bubble and heliport structures: both transfer some of their aerial lightness to the imposing, massive Lingotto. The entire Lingotto project lasted for some twenty years, and it embodies the spirit of a true architectural adventure for me.

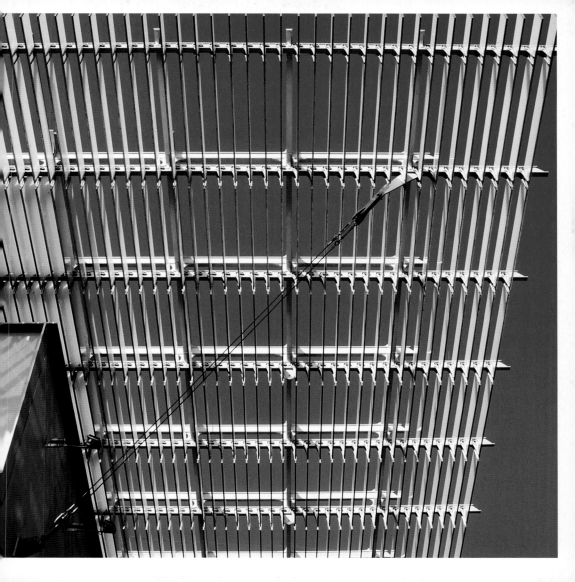

Re-development of the Genoa Old Harbour

The Old Harbour renovation in my hometown of Genoa was a huge responsibility for me. To celebrate the 500th anniversary of America's discovery by Genoese sailor Christopher Columbus, the municipality organized an international exhibition in a derelict section of the port. Apart from having to find new uses for a lot of vacant space, we were offered the fantastic opportunity to reintegrate a whole urban fragment with the city permanently.

Historically, the harbour has been the focal point of Genoa, and the city's successive expansions tended to unfurl around it. Strangely, despite this close relationship, the port was isolated from the rest of the city by various buildings and structures such as, in turn, ramparts, warehouses, custom barriers and eventually, in the 1960s, an elevated motorway. A thorough masterplan by us reorganized the whole site so as to turn it into a real public area: it aimed to transform an industrial area into the window of the city, to connect the port to the city. We had to imagine what the area would need to be or not be – many requirements that made us feel like we were performing urban surgery. While a number of warehouses were torn down, the most beautiful were thoroughly restored and transformed into public spaces with either cultural or leisure functions: among them, the historic 'Cotton Warehouse' that became a music, cinema, exhibition space and congress complex.

We also designed additions that were intended to harmonize with the spirit of the port. The aquarium, in the shape of a ship, celebrates the secular relationship between Genoa, the seas and the great discoveries. A derrick crane sculpture was also erected, quickly becoming the symbol of the Old Harbour.

More recently, on what quickly became Genoa's favourite promenade and piazza, palm trees were planted, and a bubble, a delicate structure of glass and steel filled with plants, was assembled on a bank by the aquarium.

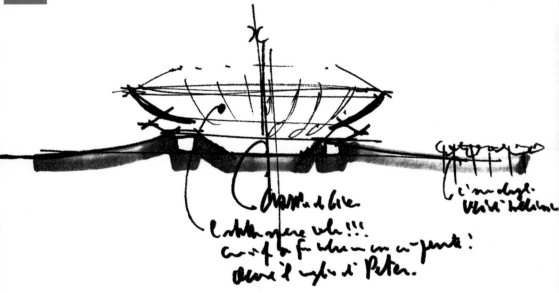

San Nicola Football Stadium

My indifference towards football is quite uncharacteristic of an Italian man. But in 1987, when Italy was awarded the role of hosting the 1990 World Cup, we were commissioned to design the 60,000-seat San Nicola Football Stadium in Bari. This was an excellent opportunity to finally acquire an interest in our national sport. It was also a great chance to develop what many stadiums then lacked – spectator safety and the drastic limitation of risk factors. Perhaps being new to the world of football provided me with some special insight into these issues.

The Stadium lies in the gentle, sunny plains of Puglia, largely surrounded by vineyards and grass. From a distance, it looks like a spaceship that has landed outside the city, on a hardly perceptible crater. This sensation is even more dramatic at night when it is illuminated.

The Stadium is divided into twenty-six petal-shaped reinforced-concrete sections: between each an independent staircase leads directly outside. The major overall requirements were visibility, to allow spectators to enjoy a game thoroughly, and a two-fold separation of the crowd, to spot safety exits immediately in case of emergency. Separation is vital, first because in life-threatening situations it limits the spread of panic, and because supporters of opposing teams do not have access to each other's area. The seats are horizontally separated in two sections, the upper and lower tiers of the stands. The second, vertical separation is generated by the wide openings between each petal.

Although these concrete petals are the result of massive engineering productions, their elliptical shape naturally conveys a feeling of lightness. When 60,000 cheering spectators fill the Stadium, it is a vibrant place, but it also retains a strong feeling of peace, generated by openness and visibility. This not only adds to the sense of security experienced by the Stadium's audience, it represents a typical example of the way we approach a building, playing with lightness and fighting with gravity.

125

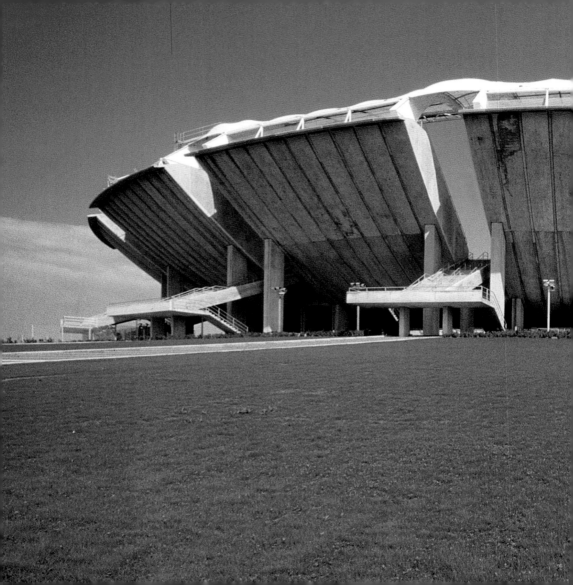

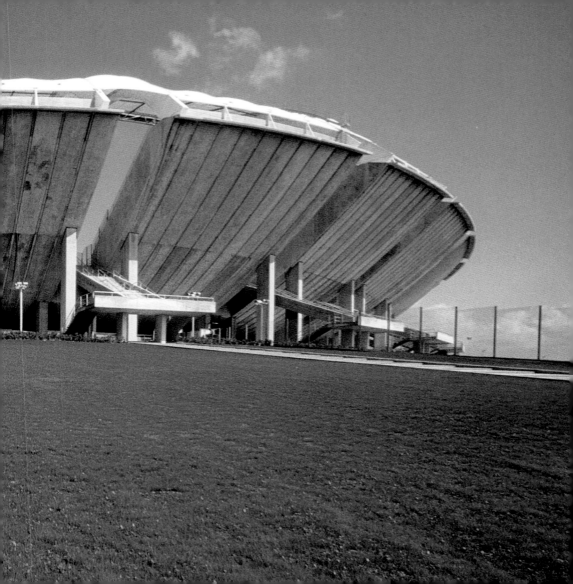

Osaka

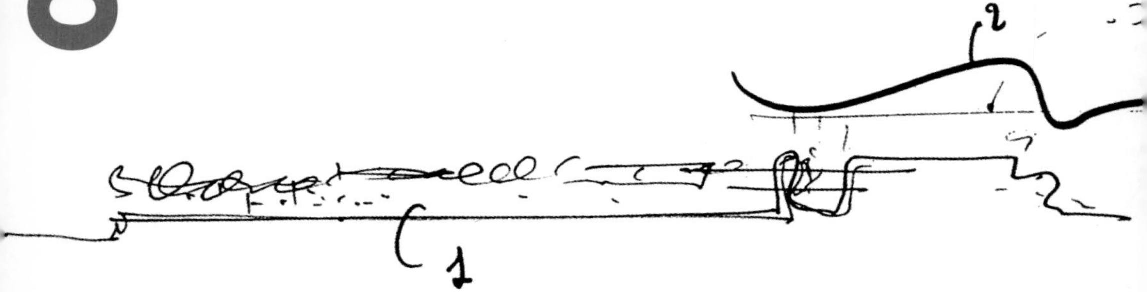

Japan

Kansai International Airport Terminal

Before starting any design, planning or study for a project, it is vital to visit and understand the site. Feeling its atmosphere and surroundings helps to lay down the general idea and philosophy, and subsequently the basic appearance. One day the challenging setting happened to be the open sea, in the Bay of Osaka. The project was the terminal building for Japan's forthcoming main airport, Kansai International. Owing to the lack of space and national regulations, it was decided that the airport would be located on a gigantic artificial island, designed by a team of engineers.

The aerodynamic shape of the terminal was generated by its immediate surroundings: waves and wind. Notwithstanding the size of the building, which is 1.7 km (1 mile) in length, its appearance is light, almost ethereal. Seen from above, one cannot help but think of a glider.

One central element of the building is the roof structure, composed of some 82,400 identical, computer-processed stainless-steel panels. Reflected sunlight and the proximity of the sea give the roof an ever-changing silvery appearance. In its section, the roof is an imperfect undulating wave: streams of air flow along this shape, making natural ventilation possible. The rather thin cover of the terminal is supported on internal beams, a skeleton whose shape matches the curves of the roof.

The simple, light shape of the building is in striking contrast with the fact that it constitutes an extraordinarily precise instrument. It is designed not only to resist earthquakes and subsequent tidal waves, but also to accommodate some 100,000 travellers per day. Inside the terminal, the curved ceiling is relatively high, whereas its width is quite constrained: this results in long corridor views, designed to create a combined feeling of space and security, significantly increasing travellers' comfort. Lengthwise, and on both sides of the larger structure in the middle of the terminal, huge bay openings look on to the tarmac, the sea and the sky, adding a sense of space. Surprisingly enough, building such a complex 'small city' in the middle of nowhere took only thirty-eight months.

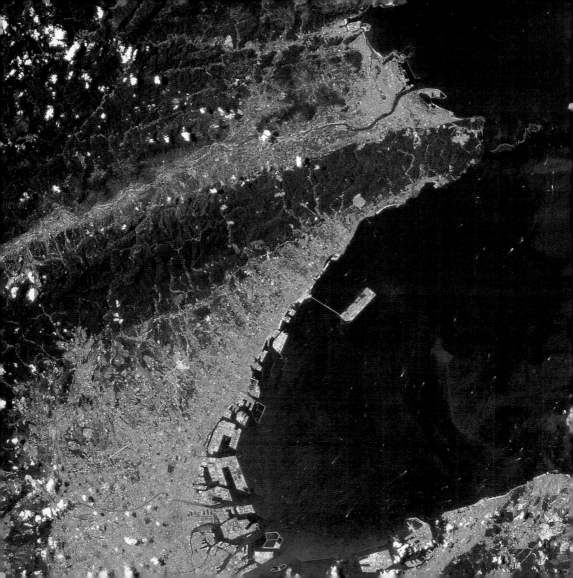

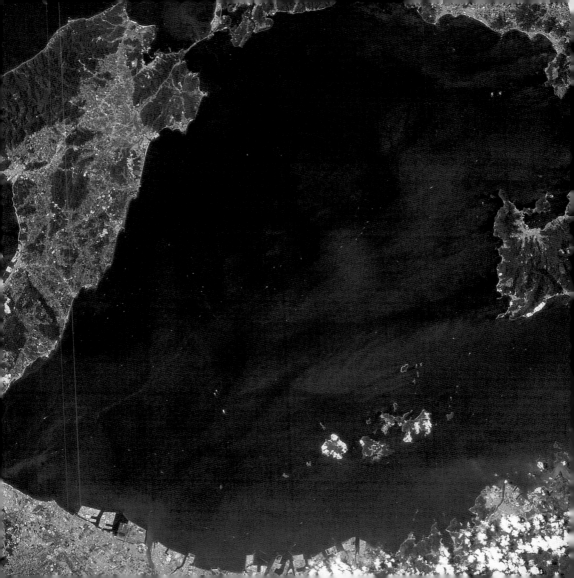

Punta Nave Genoa

Italy

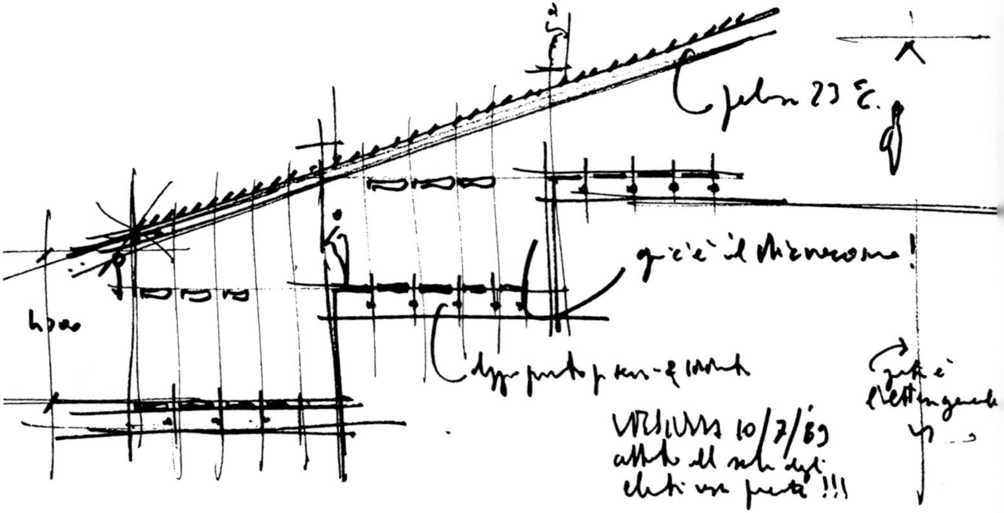

Renzo Piano Building Workshop

The relationship with my architectural projects is almost symbiotic. Being on site feels like home: this feeling persists even when the completed project has a life of its own. This could not be more the case than in Punta Nave, outside Genoa, which has been our Italian office since the early 1990s. Having spent a considerable part of the last thirty-five years working around the world, I always needed a retreat, a port in my home town. The opportunity to build a studio between the mountains of Liguria and the Mediterranean Sea, on the amazingly beautiful Italian Riviera, was not to be missed. In Paris, my second base since the Beaubourg days, I love the movement and the buzz, an urban social rivalry and all that a metropolis has to offer. All this is balanced with the silence, the beauty offered by Punta Nave, triggering both contemplation and creativity.

Punta Nave was conceived as a faithful replica of the traditional Ligurian-coast flower greenhouse. Composed of five terraced levels, it is a genuine glasshouse with a timber structure. At night, the studio resembles a magic lantern, standing between the dark sea and the garden. The garden is a major feature of the project: vegetation is luxuriant (both inside and outside) and most species found around the Mediterranean are here under the shadows of olive and palm trees. An elevator in the form of a glass box connects not only the studio and the outside world, but also all the natural elements of Punta Nave.

We all work in a single open space to the rhythm of the day. The light of the sky quickly became our natural clock. The sea can be seen from virtually everywhere you sit in the studio. The lowest terraced floor houses the model workshop, where experiments on shapes and materials are conducted.

Punta Nave is a declaration of love, a homage to the sea, to vegetation, to my roots. Most Italians have an enduring faithfulness to where they come from, and nothing is better than when clients, collaborators, and students from all over the world claim Punta Nave as their Italian home too.

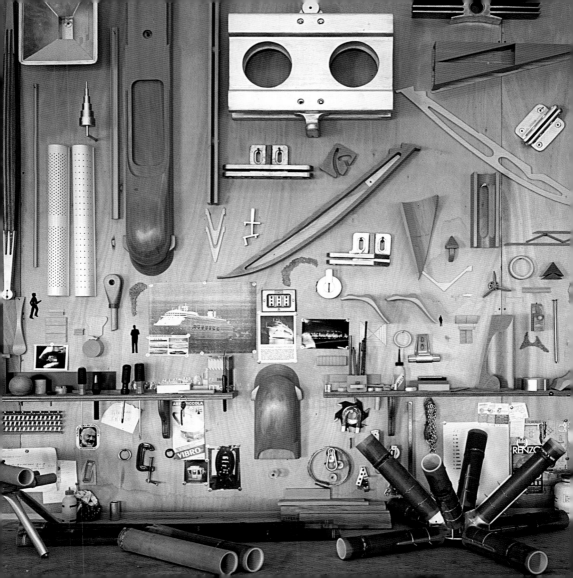

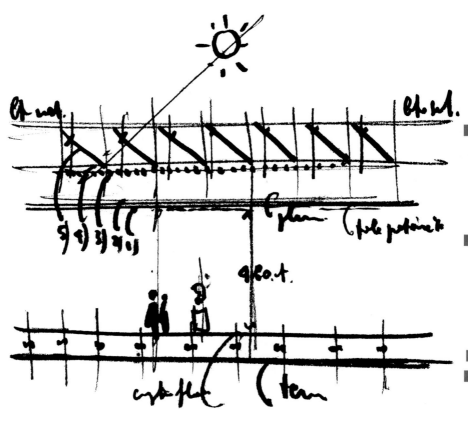

Beyeler Foundation Museum

A few years after completing the Menil Collection, we were contacted by the Swiss art collector Ernst Beyeler, who also expressed a wish to display his collection in his own public gallery. Both his approach and his personality differed from Madame de Menil's, as did his requirements, but the pleasure in giving birth to such a personal project, to confront different points of view, was the same. The settings were also radically different: one was Houston, USA, the other was Switzerland, in a much smaller park, in a denser urban area surrounding the Villa Berower, on the outskirts of Basel.

The museum is made up of four parallel walls of equal length, running along the wall enclosing the property. The three corridors created generate the exhibition spaces. The stone used resembles the typical red sandstone of the area, but this variety, which is more weather-resistant, actually comes from Argentina. The building, long and thin, looks light, notwithstanding the rocky appearance of the walls.

The roof is another main characteristic of the project: it lets the light from the sun at its zenith pour inside the galleries, a feature dear to Mr Beyeler. It is composed of layers of glass, some sloping so that the light is filtered. The roof, kept up by an invisible metal structure over the museum, and seeming to float, is designed to dramatically add to the project's impression of lightness. This roof structure has been reinterpreted and adapted for subsequent projects, such as the Giovanni and Marella Agnelli Art Gallery in Turin.

Inside, the rooms are kept simple and pure. Mr Beyeler asked us to play with ponds of water and vegetation, giving the impression that they invade the building, reinforcing the feeling of peace and purity. Galleries have white walls and wooden floors: kept as simple as possible, they leave all the attention to the paintings and sculptures, which are the main protagonists of the place, together with nature outside. The museum is light, pure and simple, giving visitors a sense of peace.

173

186

Jean-Marie Tjibaou Cultural Center

As architects, we are lucky to get the chance to collaborate closely with specialists such as engineers, landscape designers, musical experts and even anthropologists. Developing the Jean-Marie Tjibaou Cultural Center meant working with a variety of professionals, on a remote and beautiful Pacific island, and also discovering the thousand-year-old Kanak culture.

The Center lies on a narrow strip of land by the lagoon, outside Nouméa. Immersed in an ocean of vegetation comprising a natural reserve, ten huts were erected, interpreting traditional Kanak housing. With heights varying from 20 to 28 metres (66 to 92 feet), the huts symbolize Kanak traditions and beliefs, and also the practicality of their craft. Understanding accurately a new culture and representing it through all of its dimensions was a huge task. The worst mistake, which would have been easy to commit, would have been a colonial celebration of this culture, an Occidental interpretation.

With each hut connected by a footpath, the place kept most of its natural, peaceful appearance and rhythm. Elements such as wind, water, light and plants inspired the design of the huts and they bring them alive. The stylized huts, made of iroko wood, have an apparently light structure, and are bent towards the sky. The huts, the home of many Kanak festivals and celebrations, house cultural functions – temporary and permanent exhibitions, an auditorium, an amphitheatre – but also offices, a library and studios for traditional activities. Inside the huts simplicity is the rule. Elegant and discreet materials are used: glass, wood flooring and steel. This, and the modern approach of the hut interiors are in contrast to their more traditional external appearances. Based on Kanak building techniques, and combined with engineering studies, a second skin was developed in their structure to give internal natural ventilation.

Working in a remote part of the world, in such a natural, beautiful setting, and being immersed in a radically different and fascinating culture, is a life-changing experience, for which we can only be grateful.

187

Amsterdam

The Netherlands

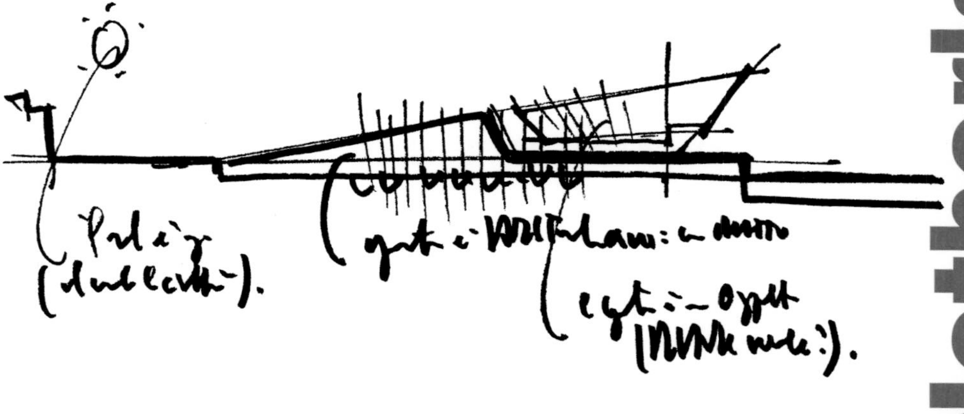

NEMO

The site chosen for NEMO (the National Centre for Science and Technology) was unusual – a small slot of land, right in the middle of Amsterdam's famous port. The shape of the building was generated by its immediate surroundings whereby the museum sits next to the sea on three sides, and, thanks to underwater foundations, it literally floats above the entrance to a pre-existing road tunnel. My passion for boats and sailing is not a secret and in the project, which is dedicated to technology, we dared to use the shape of a ship's bows for the structure. The museum does not pretend to be a piece of the city, but it integrates itself and belongs firmly to the harbour landscape.

The roof was given another specific, urban function: it was decided it would become a public area. A sloping piazza was quite a new concept in a city and a country where the land is, without exception, flat. Visitors access this terrace from inside the museum, whereas passers-by come and admire the view over Amsterdam's oldest areas from a large, long staircase leading from the port up to the top of the museum. This access ramp, together with the base of the building, is made of brick, the traditional material of Amsterdam.

Thanks to its signature shape and its size the museum is visible from anywhere in the port. Its colour too makes it visible from far away. The facade is clad in copper panels whose atmospheric elements make its colour vary from green to a nice shade of turquoise.

This was quite a challenging project, in terms of both its general appearance and its location. It was rewarding when the inhabitants of Amsterdam, unafraid of such an avant-garde design, quickly adopted the place, both for its purpose and for the view, and thought of the project a part of their city. There seems to be a lot in common between people who have grown up in a city port, whether it is in northern or southern Europe.

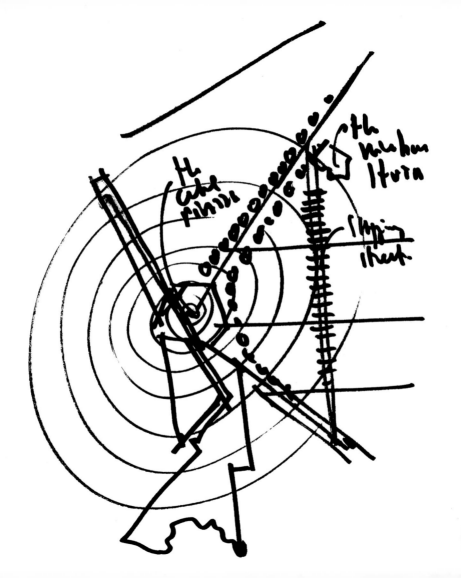

Potsdamer Platz Reconstruction

After German reunification, we won an international competition to rebuild Potsdamer Platz. The weight of responsibility was huge. Architecture and urbanism were intertwined on a gigantic site in the heart of one of Europe's largest capitals. We were all impressed by the fact that we were working on this project, helping to mend the dramatic consequences of history. Potsdamer Platz, once the heart of Berlin's social and cultural life, was entirely destroyed during the bombing of the Second World War. When the city was partitioned, it stood in the middle of a no-man's land through which the infamous Wall was erected.

The first task was to develop a masterplan of the zone to reconnect the area to the former east and west sides of the Wall, with its radically different existing buildings on each side. Potsdamer Platz was intended to be a bridge to reunite Berlin. We were helped by a surviving street, Alte Potsdamer Strasse, whose trees, surprisingly, were still standing, and which became the spine of the project: the street now ends at a smaller square we created, terminating in the theatre and casino complex foyer.

Water lies near the surface in Berlin (foundations for the site were epically dug underwater), so a pond was set up behind the theatre and along the Debis Tower and Building, the new headquarters of Daimler Chrysler, who commissioned the project. Terracotta is one of our favourite materials, and it became a common feature to the buildings we constructed on Potsdamer Platz. Its texture changes with the elements and the greenery, combined with glass, helps unify the site.

The Platz was designed as a multi-purpose area. It includes housing complexes hiding other more private piazzas, and an Imax cinema with a large glazed bay behind in the form of a massive moonlike sphere. At the tip of the Platz, towards former East Berlin, is a triangular office skyscraper made of glass. This whole project was a human adventure for all the nationalities represented on the worksite: its opening was celebrated with much joy and emotion.

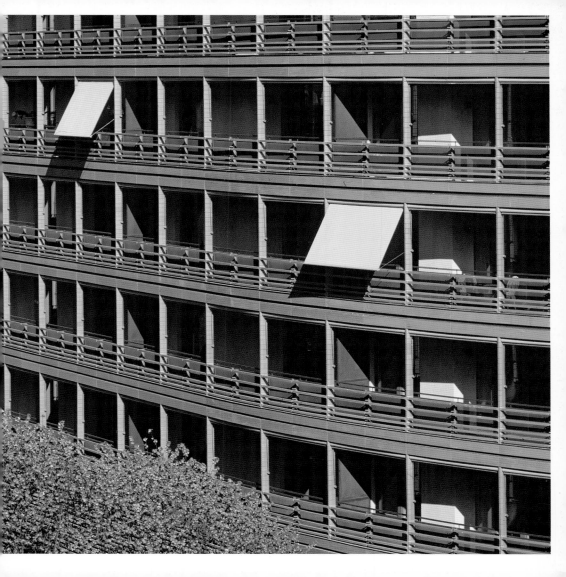

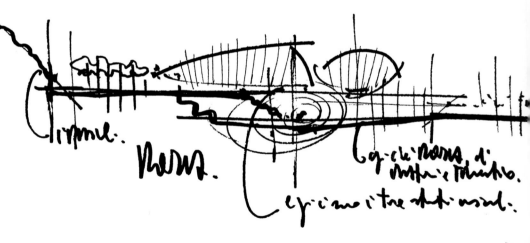

'Parco della Musica' Auditorium

The 'Parco della Musica' Auditorium can be described as a musical instrument in itself. Everything here was conceived with music in mind. Collaboration over thirty years with a large number of music professionals from various fields has been an extremely valuable education, and the auditorium is one fruit of this.

The first challenge of the auditorium, though, was urbanistic. Building such a project in Rome's dense historic centre was impossible so the site chosen lies outside the central area, an artificial fracture in the urban landscape. The whole project, a piece of town created *ex-nihilo*, is immersed in greenery and so has become a healing element. Its location near existing transport and sports infrastructure also makes it possible to accommodate and manage large movements of people.

Visible from far away, the three concert halls, each different in size, now constitute a striking reference point in the area. Conceived as true musical boxes, their beetle shape is the result of studies to ensure perfect sound reverberation. They are separated to make soundproofing easy. They appear light, and seem to levitate slightly above ground, despite their massiveness and lead roofing (whose colour varies from grey to green according to light and weather). We took advantage of the space between them to create a central square, a gathering point, which becomes the stage of a 3,000-seat open-air amphitheatre. Shows and concerts are held here, making it the unofficial fourth hall of the auditorium. The piazza is a favourite theme that recurs in many of our projects. A major urban feature in Italy, it is the heart of a community. There is an outdoor museum, also housing a 4th-century AD Roman villa which was excavated on the site.

The three halls have capacities of 2,800, 1,200 and 700 seats respectively. Their acoustics are adjustable thanks to mobile stage planes, panels and curtains, and seating arrangements. These allow the fine-tuning of reverberation times and make it possible to host a wider range of concerts and performances than a traditional hall.

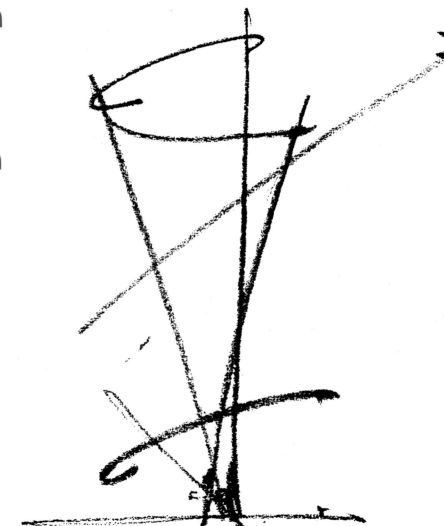

Sydney

Australia

Aurora Place

Perhaps it is because I was brought up by the Mediterranean Sea that I was breathless when I first discovered Sydney. Its bay is beautiful beyond words, and the sea is a constant element in the city's life. The skyline by the harbour is simply spectacular. The prospect of building a high-rise office and a residential tower there (for the Lend Lease Development Corporation) was irresistible.

Our project matches the intensely modern, urban character of the site in Sydney's historic district. There were, however, strict conditions to consider, including respect for the harmony of the area and for the neighbouring Opera House, the city's true architectural symbol.

Although it was to have forty-four floors, rising to 200 metres (655 feet), we wanted the tower to be as light, as little imposing as possible. The core is covered in a delicate second-skin glass facade, enveloping the building like a rising sail, extending above the volume itself. We adopted the same principle for the smaller seventeen-floor residential tower next to it.

The main characteristics of this project derive from its friendliness towards users and the environment. Winter gardens and terraces were included from the start. Thanks to a screen-printing process, the glass skin regulates sunlight and temperature, reducing the need for air-conditioning.

Although it has skyscraper proportions, we wanted this project to remain on a human scale, to take into account the needs of the people, offering them more than convenient working and living conditions. We wanted it to have a fantastic urban quality, while remaining light and simple.

Parma

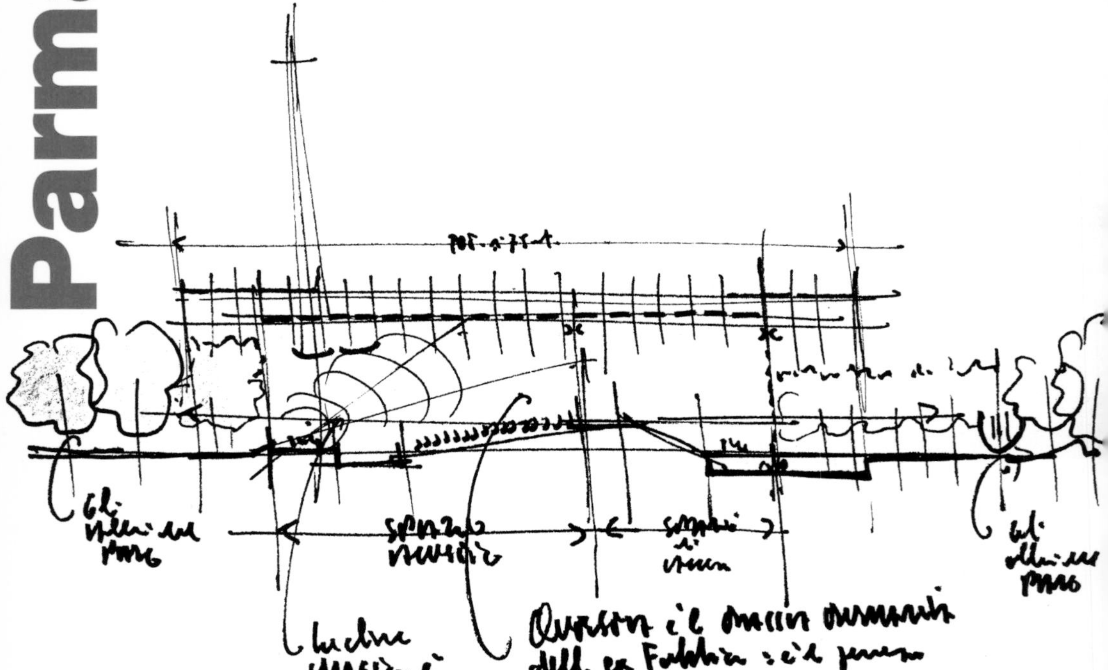

Italy

Niccolò Paganini Auditorium

We are always looking for architectural challenges. The more complicated a project appears to be the better, as it will promote experiment and innovation. It keeps one's mind young. This was the case when we were asked to perform quite an unusual conversion in Parma: transforming a former sugar factory into an auditorium. The proposal was odd, but it made sense, and we were glad to take on another quest.

The factory stands in a former industrial estate, now a well-established park, near Parma's historic centre. Two factors helped the outcome of the project greatly: the size of the factory, which conformed to basic acoustic proportions, and the location in the park, which simplified the sound-proofing process. Of the original structure, we kept the two main walls along the length of the building and the roof structure (which was thoroughly restored). The transverse curtain walls were demolished and subsequently replaced by three glass walls. From outside, one has a view throughout the 90 metre (295 foot) long building. From any of the 780 seats in the hall, and from the foyer, there are views over the park.

We enter the auditorium from the south end, into an open-roofed space. A staircase leads to the entrance, set in the first glass wall. At the entrance, the gentle sloping level (carrying the seating stalls) goes down to the end of the hall, where the 250 metre (820 foot) stage stands. Adjustable acoustic panels fly above the stage where they adapt in function according to the performance. The auditorium allows the audience to experience both music and nature simultaneously through a light and simple structure.

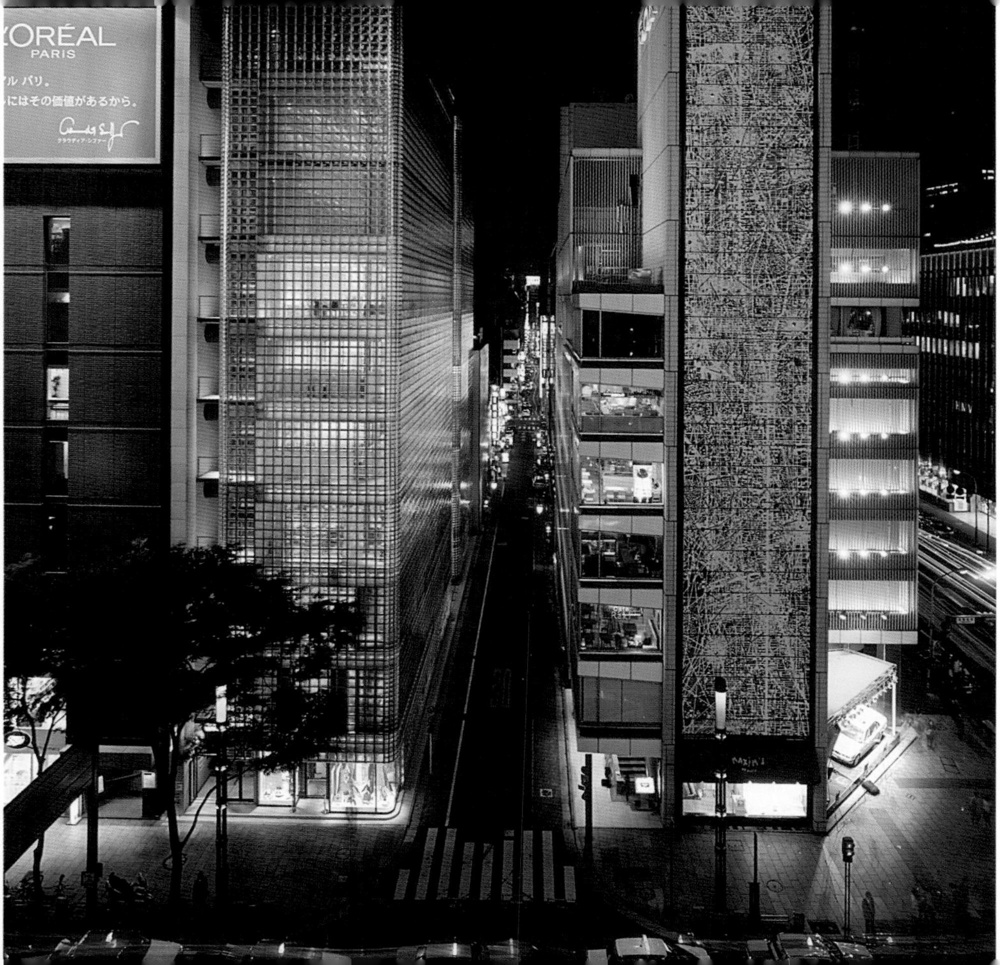
ORÉAL
PARIS

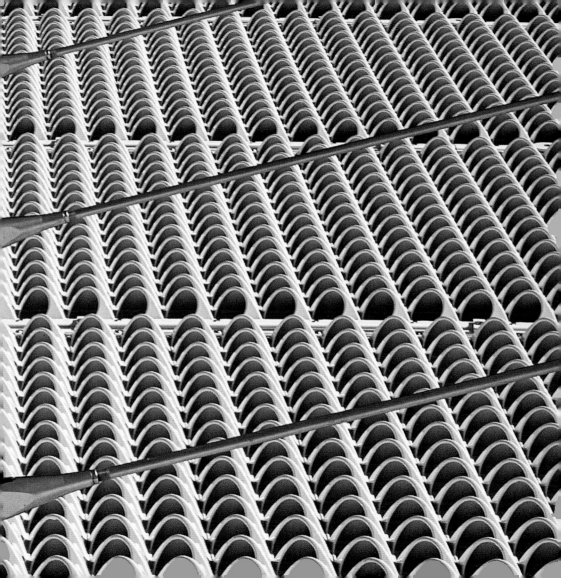

Renzo Piano Building Workshop
Paris and Genoa

Senior Partners

Mark Carroll
Philippe Goubet
Giorgio Grandi
Shunji Ishida
Flavio Marano
Bernard Plattner
Paul Vincent

Partners

Emanuela Baglietto
Giorgio Bianchi
Antoine Chaaya
Olaf de Nooyer
Donald Hart
Joost Moolhuijzen
Susanna Scarabicchi

Associates

Antonio Belvedere
Ivan Corte
Alain Gallissian
Vittorio Grassi
Domenico Magnano
William Matthews
Nayla Mecattaf
Jean-Bernard Mothes
Daniele Piano
Dominique Rat
Anne-Hélène Temenides
Vittorio Tolu
Elisabetta Trezzani

Maurits Van der Staay
Erik Volz

Consultants

Loïc Couton
Maria Salerno
Alain Vincent

Architects

Luca Battaglia
Jeremy Boon
Morten Busk Petersen
Jack Carter
David Colas
Sheila Colon
Paolo Colonna
Leonhard Coreth
Luca Dal Cerro
Kendall Doerr
Serge Drouin
Fatma Elmalipinar
Attila Eris
Stefano Giorgio-Marrano
Adam Guernier
Oliver Hempel
Pascal Hendier
Serge Joly
Torben Kajaer
Alexander Knapp
Justin Lee
Andrew McClure
Jonathan McNeal
Caroline Maxwell-Mahon

Nikola Meyer
Antonio Ng
Chi Tam Nguyên
David Patterson
Marie Pimmel
Sara Polotti
Mauro Prini
Mario Reale
Luis Reggiardo
Emilia Rossato
Julien Rousseau
Thorsten Sahlmann
Robert Sproull
Onur Teke
Brett Terpeluk
Danilo Vespier
Cristiano Zaccaria

CAD Operators

Stefano D'Atri
Giovanna Langasco
Mara Ottonello
Pierre Roscelli

Model-makers

Olivier Aubert
Fausto Cappellini
Christophe Colson
Yiorgos Kyrkos
Andrea Malgeri
Andrea Marazzi

Documentation & Archives

Stefania Canta
Chiara Casazza
Giovanna Giusto
Patricia Guyot

Administration

Cristina Calvi
Catherine Fleury
Jeanine Lottin
Antonio Porcile
Hélène Teboul

Secretarial Department

Francesca Bianchi
Daniela Cappuzzo
Fulvia Pesavento
Sylvie Romet-Milane
Tamara Tomasetto

RPBW, July 2005

...ject Credits

...1/1977
...tre Georges Pompidou
...is, France

...nt: Ministry of Cultural Affairs,
...istry of National Education

...dio Piano & Rogers

...nsultants: Ove Arup & Partners, M. Espinoza

...ntractors: GTM with Krupp, Pont-à-Mousson,
...lig, Voyer, Otis, Industrielle de Chauffage,
...nier Duval and CFEM

...1/1990
...AM
...is, France

...se One, 1971–77
...nt: Ministry of Cultural Affairs,
...istry of National Education

...dio Piano & Rogers

...nsultants: Ove Arup & Partners, M. Espinoza

...se Two, 1988–90
...nt: Ministry of Culture,
...tre Georges Pompidou, IRCAM

...zo Piano Building Workshop, architects

...nsultants: AXE IB, GEC Ingénierie, GEMO

...2/1996
...ier Brancusi Reconstruction
...is, France

...nt: Centre Georges Pompidou

...zo Piano Building Workshop, architects

...nsultants: GEC Ingénierie, INEX, Isis

...2/1987
... Menil Collection
...uston, Texas, USA

...nt: The Menil Foundation

...no & Fitzgerald, architects

...nsultants: Ove Arup & Partners,
...ne & Whaley Associates, Galewsky & Johnston,
...ensen

1992/1995
Cy Twombly Pavilion
Houston, Texas, USA

Client: The Menil Foundation

Renzo Piano Building Workshop, architects

Consultants: R. Fitzgerald & Associates,
Ove Arup & Partners, Haynes Whaley Associates,
Lockwood Andrews & Newman

1983/1986
IBM Travelling Pavilion
Travelling, Europe

Client: IBM Europe

Renzo Piano/Building Workshop/Atelier de Paris,
architects

Consultants: Ove Arup & Partners

Contractor: Calabrese Engineering S.p.a.

1983/2003
Lingotto Factory Conversion
Turin, Italy

Client: Fiat SpA + Lingotto SpA +
Pathé + Palazzo Grassi

Renzo Piano Building Workshop, architects

Consultants: Ove Arup & Partners, AI Engineering,
Fiat Engineering, Manens Intertecnica,
Prodim+Teksystem, Arup Acoustics, Müller BBM,
Peutz & Associés, PI Greco Engineering,
Davis Langdon Everest, Fiat Engineering,
GEC Ingénierie, Emmer Pfenninger Partner, RFR,
Techplan, P. Castiglioni, P. L. Cerri, ECO SpA,
F. Santolini, F. Mirenzi, CIA, Studio Vitone & Associati,
F. Levi/G. Mottino, Studio Rousset

2000/2002
The Giovanni and Marella Agnelli Art Gallery
at Lingotto
Turin, Italy

Client: Lingotto SpA + Palazzo Grassi

Renzo Piano Building Workshop, architects

Consultants: RFR, Fiat Engineering,
PI Greco Engineering, P. Castiglioni, Studio Inarco

1985/2001
Re-development of the Genoa Old Harbour
Genoa, Italy

Client: City of Genoa + Porto Antico SpA

Renzo Piano Building Workshop, architects

Phase One (Columbus International Exposition),
1985–92
Consultants: Ove Arup & Partners, L. Mascia/
D. Mascia, P. Costa, L. Lembo, V. Nascimbene,
B. Ballerini, G. Malcangi, Sidercard, M. Testone, G. F.
Visconti, Manens Intertecnica, STED, D. Commins,
Scene, P. Castiglioni, M. Semino, Cambridge Seven
Associates, Cetena, Origoni & Steiner, L. Moni

Curator for the Italian Pavilion exhibition: G. Macchi

Wind sculptures: S. Shingu

General contractor and Project Manager: Italimpianti

Phase Two, 1993–2001
Consultants: Ove Arup & Partners, Rocca-Bacci
& Associati, E. Lora, Polar Glassin System, B. Ballerini,
STED, Austin Italia, Tekne, M. Gronda, P. Nalin,
Studio Galli, P. Castiglioni, G. Marini, C. Manfreddo,
P. Varratta, Techint

1987/1990
San Nicola Football Stadium
Bari, Italy

Client: Municipality of Bari

Renzo Piano Building Workshop, architects

Consultants: M. Desvigne, Ove Arup & Partners,
M. Milan, Studio Vitone & Associati, N. Andidero,
J. Zucker, M. Belviso

1988/1994
Kansai International Airport Terminal
Osaka, Japan

Client: Kansai International Airport Co. Ltd.

Renzo Piano Building Workshop, architects
N. Okabe, senior partner in charge
in association with Nikken Sekkei Ltd.,
Aéroports de Paris, Japan Airport Consultants Inc.

Consultants: Ove Arup & Partners, Peutz & Associés,
R. J. Van Santen, RFR, David Langdon & Everest,
Futaba Quantity Surveying Co. Ltd., M. Desvigne,
K. Nyunt, Toshi Keikan Sekkei Inc.

1989/1991
Renzo Piano Building Workshop
Punta Nave, Genoa, Italy

Client: Renzo Piano Building Workshop

Renzo Piano Building Workshop, architects

Consultants: A. Bellini, L. Gattoronchieri, P. Costa,
M. Desvigne, C. Di Bartolo

1991/1997
Beyeler Foundation Museum
Riehen, Basel, Switzerland

Client: Beyeler Foundation

Renzo Piano Building Workshop, architects
in association with Burckhardt + Partner AG, Basel

Consultants: Ove Arup & Partners,
C. Burger + Partner AG, Bogenschütz AG, J. Forrer
Elektrizitäts AG, J. Wiede, Schönholzer + Stauffer

1991/1998
Jean-Marie Tjibaou Cultural Center
Nouméa, New Caledonia

Client: Agence pour le Développement
de la Culture Kanak

Renzo Piano Building Workshop, architects

Consultants: A. Bensa, Ove Arup & Partners,
Agibat MTI, GEC Ingénierie, CSTB, Scène,
Peutz & Associés, Qualiconsult, Desvigne & Dalnoky
Végétude, Intégral R. Baur

1991/2001
Banca Popolare di Lodi Headquarters
Lodi, Italy

Client: Banca Popolare di Lodi

Renzo Piano Building Workshop, architects

Consultants: M.S.C., Manens Intertecnica, Müller BI
Gierrevideo, P. Castiglioni, P. L. Cerri, F. Santolini

2/1997
MO
sterdam, The Netherlands

nt: NINT

zo Piano Building Workshop, architects

sultants: Ove Arup & Partners, D3BN, Huisman
'an Muijen BV, Peutz, Bureau voor Bouwkunde

2/2000
sdamer Platz Reconstruction
in, Germany

nt: Daimler-Chrysler AG

zo Piano Building Workshop, architects
ssociation with Christoph Kohlbecker

sultants: Ove Arup & Partners, Boll & Partners,
Dr. Falkner GmbH/Weiske & Partner, IGH,
midt-Reuter & Partner, Müller BBM,
dt & Partner, IBB Burrer, ITF Intertraffic,
er Dreiseitl, P. L. Copat, Krüger & Möhrle,
es & Sommer/Kohlbecker

4/2002
rco della Musica' Auditorium
ne, Italy

nt: City of Rome

zo Piano Building Workshop, architects

sultants: Ove Arup & Partners,
dio Vitone & Associati, Manens Intertecnica,
er Bbm, Davis Langdon & Everest, T. Gatehouse,
tin Italia, F. Zagari, E. Trabella, Tecnocons,
Cerri, Techint / Drees & Sommer

6/2000
ora Place
ney, Australia

nt: Lend Lease Development

zo Piano Building Workshop, architects

sultants: Lend Lease Design Group, Group GSA
Ltd, Ove Arup & Partners, Taylor Thomson Whitting

1997/2001
Niccolò Paganini Auditorium
Parma, Italy

Client: City of Parma

Renzo Piano Building Workshop, architects

Consultants: Müller BBM, P. Costa,
Manens Intertecnica, Paghera, Studio Galli,
Gierrevideo, Amitaf, Austin Italia, F. Santolini

1998/2001
Maison Hermès
Tokyo, Japan

Client: Hermès Japon

Renzo Piano Building Workshop, architects
in collaboration with Rena Dumas Architecture
Intérieure (Paris)

Consulting executive architect: Takenaka Corporation
Design Department

Consultants: Ove Arup & Partners, Syllabus, Delphi,
Ph. Almon, R. Labeyrie, K. Tanaka, Atelier 10/
N. Takata, ArchiNova Associates

Sculpture: S. Shingu

1999/2003
The Nasher Sculpture Center
Dallas, Texas, USA

Client: The Nasher Foundation

Renzo Piano Building Workshop, architects

Consultants: Peter Walker & Partners,
Ove Arup & Partners, Interloop A/D, Beck Architecture

General Contractor: HCBeck

Selected Bibliography

Renzo Piano, Magda Arduino, Mario Fazio
Antico è bello, il recupero della città
Editori Laterza, Bari 1980

Gianpiero Donin
Renzo Piano. Pezzo per pezzo
Casa del libro, Bari 1982

Massimo Dini
Renzo Piano. Progetti e architetture 1964–1983
Electa, Milan 1983
Renzo Piano. Architectural Projects 1964–1983
Architectural Press, London 1983

Renzo Piano
Chantier ouvert au public
Arthaud, Paris 1985

Renzo Piano
Progetti e architetture 1984–1986
Electa, Milan 1986

Renzo Piano
Renzo Piano
Editions du Centre Pompidou, Paris 1987

Renzo Piano, Richard Rogers
Du Plateau Beaubourg au Centre G. Pompidou
Editions du Centre Pompidou, Paris 1987

Umberto Eco, Federico Zeri, Renzo Piano,
Augusto Graziani
Le Isole del tesoro
Electa, Milan 1989

Renzo Piano
Renzo Piano Building Workshop 1964–1988
A+U extra edition, Tokyo 1989

Renzo Piano
Renzo Piano Buildings and Projects 1971–1989
Rizzoli International, New York 1989

Renzo Piano
**Renzo Piano Building Workshop 1964–1991,
In search of a balance**
Process Architecture, Tokyo, No.100, 1992

Carla Garbato, Mario Mastropietro
Exhibit & Design
Lybra Edizioni, Milan 1992

Peter Buchanan
**Renzo Piano Building Workshop,
Complete Works Vol.1**
Phaidon Press, London 1993

Vittorio Magnago Lampugnani
Renzo Piano. Progetti e architetture 1987–1994
Electa, Milan 1994
Renzo Piano. Architectural Projects 1987–1994
Birkhäuser, Berlin 1994

Renzo Piano
The Making of Kansai International Airport Termin
Kodansha, Tokyo 1994

Renzo Piano
**Kansai International Airport
Passenger Terminal Building**
Process Architecture, Tokyo, No.122, 1994

Renzo Piano
**Kansai International Airport
Passenger Terminal Building**
JA No.15, 1994

KIAC
**Construction of the Kansai
International Airport Terminal**
KIAC, 1995

Peter Buchanan
**Renzo Piano Building Workshop,
Complete Works Vol.2**
Phaidon Press, London 1995

Gianni Berengo Gardin
Foto Piano
Peliti Associati, Rome 1996

Renzo Piano
Giornale di Bordo
Passigli ed., Florence 1997
The Renzo Piano Logbook
Thames and Hudson, London 1997

Robert Bordaz
Entretiens avec Renzo Piano
Cercle d'art, Paris 1997

neth Frampton
zo Piano Building Workshop
Architect, No.14, A.D.A., Tokyo 1997

er Buchanan
zo Piano Building Workshop,
nplete Works Vol.3
don Press, London 1997

ert Ingersoll
ean Architects No.158
itecture & Environment Publications, Seoul 1997

zo Piano
dation Beyeler – A home for art
häuser, Basel 1998

ner Blaser
zo Piano Building Workshop – Museum Beyeler
ée Beyeler, Benteli
ag, Bern 1998

io Paternostro
oni di Piano
Ferrari, Genoa 1999

er Cinqualbre, Françoise Fromonot,
rry Paquot, Marc Bédarida
zo Piano, un regard construit
ibition catalogue)
ions du Centre Pompidou, Paris 2000

zo Piano
itekturen des Lebens
ibition catalogue)
e Cantz Verlag, Ostfildern-Ruit 2000

zo Cassigoli
esponsabilità dell'architetto
versazione con Renzo Cassigoli
sigli editori, Florence 2000

er Buchanan
zo Piano Building Workshop,
nplete Works Vol.4
don Press, London 2000

zo Piano
it of Nature – Wood Architecture Award 2000
inki, 2000 (on the occasion of the prize given
enzo Piano in September 2000)

Alban Bensa
Ethnologie & Architecture – Le centre culturel
Tjibaou – une réalisation de Renzo Piano
Adam Birò, Paris 2000

Werner Blaser
Cultural Center of the Kanak People
Birkhäuser, Basel 2001

Andrew Metcalf, Martin Van der Wal
Aurora Place – Renzo Piano Sydney
The Watermark Press, Sydney 2001

Giovanni Di Lorenzo, Mark Münzing, Karl Schlögel
Potsdamer Platz Project 1989 to 2000
Daimler Chrysler Immobilien (DCI) GmbH, Berlin 2001

Fulvio Irace, Gabriele Basilico
The Music Factory, The City of Parma's
Auditorium Paganini
Abitare Segesta, Milan 2002

Renzo Piano Building Workshop – Musica per Roma
Architecture & Music – Seven sites for music:
from the Ircam in Paris to the Auditorium in Roma
(the exhibition catalogue on the occasion
of the opening of the Auditorium in Rome)
Lybra Immagine Publications, Milan 2002

Aurora Cuito
Renzo Piano
LOFT Publications, Barcelona 2002

Emilio Pizzi
Renzo Piano
Zanichelli, Bologna 2002
Birkhäuser, Basel 2002

Maria Alessandra Segantini
Auditorium Parco della Musica
Federico Motta Editore, Milan 2004

Gigliola Ausiello, Francesco Polverino
Renzo Piano, architettura e tecnica
Clean Edizioni, Naples 2004

Renzo Piano
Renzo Piano & Building Workshop
Exhibition catalogue, Tormena Editore, Genoa 2004

Photography Credits

Arcaid
Gabriele Basilico
Gianni Berengo-Gardin
Niggi Brauning
Richard Bryant
Enrico Cano
Centre Georges Pompidou
Michel Denancé
Richard Einzig
FI.L.S.E.
Fregoso & Basalto
Dennis Gilbert
Stefano Goldberg
John Gollings
Donald Hart
Paul Hester
Hichey & Robertson
Alistair Hunter
Aldo Ippoliti
Shunji Ishida
Kawatetsu
Yutaka Kinumaki
Moreno Maggi
Georges Meguerditchias
Studio Merlo
Emanuela Minetti
Mattia Morgavi
Vincent Mosch
Glenn Murcutt
Olaf de Nooyer
Palladium; Barbara Burg/Oliver Schuh
Publifoto
Christian Richters
Aereophoto Schipol
Shinkenchi-ku-sha
Sky front's
Ben Smusz
Haskins Squire
Martin Van Der Wal
William Vassal
Paul Vincent

Acknowledgements

Renzo Piano Building Workshop would like to thank the following people: Giorgio Bianchi, Francesca Bianchi, Stefania Canta, Chiara Casazza and Patric Guyot at RPBW; Aymeric Lorenté for his assistance with the text; Annalisa Treccani and Marta Biondi for their assistance with the design.

Prizes and Acknowledgements

1978   Union Internationale des Architects Honorary Fellowship, Mexico City, Mexico

1981   Compasso d'Oro Award, Milan, Italy
AIA (American Institute of Architecture) Honorary Fellowship, USA

1984   Commandeur des Arts et des Lettres Award, Paris, France

1985   Legion d'Honneur, Paris, France
RIBA Honorary Fellowship in London, UK

1989   RIBA Royal Gold Medal for Architecture, UK
Cavaliere di Gran Croce award by the Italian Government, Rome, Italy

1990   Honorary Doctorship, Stuttgart University, Germany
Kyoto Prize, Inamori Foundation, Kyoto, Japan

1991   Neutra Prize, Pomona, California, USA

1992   Honorary Doctorship, Delft University, The Netherlands

1993   American Academy of Arts and Sciences, Fellow, London, UK

1994   American Academy of Arts and Letters, Honorary Fellowship, USA
Arnold W. Brunner Memorial Prize, USA
Chevalier, l'Ordre National du Mérite, Paris, France
Goodwill Ambassador of Unesco for Architecture
Premio Michelangelo in Rome, Italy
Prize for Actuactiones temporales de Urbanismo y Arquitectura
from the Ayuntamiento de Madrid, Spain

1995   Art Prize of the Akademie der Künste, Berlin, Germany
Praemium Imperiale, Tokyo, Japan
Erasmus Prize, Amsterdam, The Netherlands

1996   Premio Capo Circeo, Rome, Italy

1998   The Pritzker Architecture Prize, The White House, Washington DC, USA

1999   Architect of the National Academy of San Luca, Rome, Italy

2000   Officier, Ordre National de la Légion d'Honneur, Paris, France
Leone d'Oro for the career, Venice, Italy
Spirit of Nature Wood Architecture Award, Helsinki, Finland
Premio Leonardo, Palazzo del Quirinale, Rome, Italy

2001   Wexner Prize, Wexner Center for the Arts, Columbus, Ohio, USA

2002   Honorary Doctor of Fine Arts Degree, Pratt Institute, New York, USA
Médaille D'Or UIA (International Union of Architects), Berlin, Germany
Michelangelo Antonioni for the Arts, Rome Auditorium, Italy

2003   Gold Medal for Italian Architecture, 'Triennale' of Milan, Italy
'Una vita nella musica – Artur Rubinstein', Venice, Italy

2004   Grifo d'Oro, Comune di Genova, Genoa, Italy
Italy – America Chamber of Commerce Business Cultural Award for 2003,
New York, USA

Phaidon Press Limited
Regent's Wharf
All Saints Street
London N1 9PA

Phaidon Press Inc.
180 Varick Street
New York, NY 10014

www.phaidon.com

First published 2004
First reprint 2005
Second reprint 2005
Third reprint 2005
© 2004 Phaidon Press Limited
ISBN 0 7148 4341 5

A CIP catalogue record for this book
is available from the British Library.

Designed by Franco Origoni and Anna Steiner
Printed in China